THE
AUDACITY
TO PERSEVERE

My Journey of Survival, Resilience, and Redemption

Rev. Dr. Charles Williams

Major Dr. Williams

Charles Williams

ISBN 978-1-63630-423-6 (Paperback)
ISBN 978-1-63630-424-3 (Digital)

Covenant Books, Inc.
11661 Hwy 707
Murrells Inlet, SC 29576
www.covenantbooks.com

CONTENTS

FOREWORD

It was literally the end of 1995 when I met Charles, through a mutual friend. It was a time of refocusing my life through a turbulent separation and spiritual awakening. It was the beginning of a journey with an incredible determine man with challenges he faced and would continue to face head on. Yet I didn't know the strength, perseverance and determination he held so deeply over the years. But God revealed we were meant to be together.

I'm so proud and honored to write this foreword because first hand I saw the struggle and the victories as we walked this journey together over the last 23 years. I know all things are possible when you lean on, trust in and obey God's direction.

Through this book, it will encourage, it will have you look back over your life at the choices you've made and remind yourself it is never too late for God's promises to be fulfilled. Remember God never left you nor forsaken you. We are all God's workmanship.

Love you babe wife,
Carol D. Williams

Growing up as the oldest son, my father worked hard at everything, he set out to do. I remember dad being a God-fearing man of God. If, I need him, I knew I could find him at work, church, school or working his second job. My dad worked full time as computer operator, programmer, owned his own business cleaning carpets and upholstery went school full-time and served his church as ordain elder. He took, my brother us alone with many times so we could learn how to work and care for own, families, when we grow up. Even, dad had time enough time to attend our sport games, while in school. He didn't miss a game for me or my brother, Jeremi. Plus, he coached my baseball team, on weekends. What a dad. He always told us, as his dad told him, "work hard and everything, will be alright." To this dad me and my brother and sisters are hard workers, and will not take no, for an answer. Lastly, each of us are teaching our children to work hard, at whatever you go, to do.

Charles E. Williams II
oldest son

Growing up I flew to Chicago regularly to visit my dad and brothers. Being the youngest of three, I was my dad's shadow. Whether it was going to church, work, or a community event, we were there. My dad didn't meet a stranger and was pleased to help whoever was in need. Over the years he has assisted people spiritually, financially, emotionally, physically, and mentally.

All while never being reluctant to share his testimony with, all while encouraging others to keep pushing forward and keep GOD first.

Daddy, I am extremely proud of you and all that you have achieved. Thank you for always being there for me. You have taught me about GOD, love, and to keeping striving for better. I love you.

Sincerely,
Charnita D. Williams
Daddy's Girl, youngest daughter

I was in high school when my mom met Charles Williams. My godmother introduced them. My mom was excited yet nervous for her first date, but look what God had blessed her with. He is a man of God and family. Through all of his struggles he has shown perseverance. If this book teaches you anything it is how to persevere. It will teach you that anything is possible with God.

Megan J. McKay
Step Daughter

For as long as I can remember, my father has been a God fearing, hardworking, dedicated, family man. Our family has been through many trials and tribulations in our past. My father made sure that my brother and I had everything we ever needed and wanted. He would work as long and as much as he needed to so he could provide for our family. I remember my dad serving with the Salvation Army, as an employee and officer/pastor. Plus, going to school fulltime and running his own business, carpet and upholstery cleaning service. Also, he was always there for any sports, we played in school. The man that I got to watch growing up was my hero and one that was always there. My brother and I knew that it was hard for him to do, but he never complained or let us down one time. My father's life changed forever when he met Carol. I think she was the stability in his life that he needed. He needed someone caring, understanding, God fearing, and beautiful. Carol is all of those things plus more. You will hear stories where my father persevered through many situations during his life. I have been there to see how my father has kept God first, and his family next. All the lives that my dad has impacted through his work with the Salvation Army, Outreach Church of God in Christ, and counseling will go on forever.

Jeremi D. Williams
Youngest Son

INTRODUCTION

I'm a high school dropout. I never made it past the ninth grade. The reason why is complicated and will be explored throughout the telling of my story of perseverance. But one of the short versions of why I am a high school dropout is because I wanted to pursue ministry; I wanted to follow the call I felt was on my life.

When I was fifteen years old, I dropped out of high school and followed my older brother from Chicago to New York where we worked in ministry. At that time, I had only earned one-half of credit in high school.

My life's story is a testimony that your beginning doesn't have to set the tone for your entire life. At the writing of this book, I am a newly retired sixty-five-year-old Salvation Army officer, minister, and chaplain. As an adult, I earned my GED, a bachelor's degree, two master's degrees, and a doctorate. It wasn't easy and didn't come without sacrifice, but God carried me all the way. From my journey, I've learned so much, most of which involved perseverance and learning to love myself. While I'd identified as a Christian since an early age, I have also learned many lessons that have shaped my faith and helped me grow as a Christian and a servant leader to God's people.

The words in this book are meant to help you, the reader, hopefully learn and grow as I did. Life hasn't been easy; it has not been filled with all mountaintop victories. I've hit rock bottom and questioned my beliefs, but God has sustained me and restored me. I want to share my story to encourage others to keep going, to keep growing, and to keep trusting in God's amazing sovereignty and ability. Dreams can be attained no matter your age or education level. I'm a living witness. From high school dropout to doctorate degree holder, I am an ordained elder, board-certified chaplain, and a Salvation

Army officer. God has been good to me. God has redeemed me and restored much of what I sacrificed and gave up when I didn't know any better.

My story can be read by many different audiences. While serving with the Salvation Army, I have been before many different audiences. I served at two Harbor Lights as chaplain or counselor and corps officer or pastor. Those who have been addicted and lost all they had, including their families, can rebuild their lives, one step at a time. As corps officers and being part of social services at each location, we served clients from every walk of life. As chaplain in Omaha, I served twenty-six in-house programs. There were shelters for mentally ill clients, single women and men, VA clients, traffic victims, abused women, and many others. Anyone in similar circumstances may benefit from my story of perseverance. In addition, there are many officers and employees who can benefit as I did. Lastly, those who have lost hope and can't find their way—older adults who think that it's too late to recover and rise again and younger people looking for direction—I believe all of you can benefit from this story. In addition, to anyone who has gone through divorce and needs to rebuild their lives and make a new start, this book is for you. And hopefully the list of benefactors will go on and on.

CHAPTER 1

My Beginnings and Foundation

My name is Charles E. Williams. I was born on April 12, 1954, in the small town of Leland, Mississippi, to Earlis Williams Jr. and Ruthie Mae Williams. I was the youngest child of seven. My brothers and sisters, in order of birth, are Rose, Delores, Robert, Carolyn, Lamar, and Ray.

My father was a hard worker; he was raised by sharecroppers who worked from sunup to sundown. My dad couldn't read or write because farming was all he and his parents knew. They did move north to Chicago once I was born in the '50s. My immediate family as well as my grandparents migrated to the West Side of Chicago in hopes of a better life than they had in the Jim Crow South.

Because of his work ethic, my dad found a job quickly in Chicago. He worked at Dayton Electric, making fans and air conditioners. His hard work helped him become foreman after a couple of years. He also got the opportunity to hire some of his brothers and sisters at his job, and some of my brothers and sisters worked there too.

"Work hard and everything will be all right" was the main message I heard from my father. He repeated this mantra regularly and proved it by moving up in his job and gaining enough influence to hire others.

I didn't hear anything about education as I was growing up. Hard work had gotten my father, who dropped out of school in third grade, further in life than his father. Hard work was all my father knew and all he ever preached. He did all right for a man who couldn't sign his name on papers. I still remember him having my sisters read and sign whatever he needed.

My mother had a bit more education than my father. She completed eighth grade but didn't go to high school. She stayed home and took care of her children. She stayed at home with all of her children except me. By the time we moved to Chicago, my mom got a job outside of the house. This made me feel abandoned and lonely at a young age. I felt like I had missed out on the special nurturing my mother had been able to give to my siblings. I wanted the attention and time my mother had for my siblings.

Like my father, my mom also believed in hard work. In fact, once we were all a certain age, we had to get jobs; and my mom took some of the money we earned to use for household expenses. As a freshman—the short time I stayed in school—I worked at the airport and had a paper route. My mom got us permits to work earlier than the legal working age; I was tall for my age so people thought I was older than I was. She was serious about developing our work ethic as early as possible.

Ministry in Chicago, Then Moved to New York

I guess that's one reason school just didn't appeal to me. I dropped out of high school at fifteen to follow my brother and a minister to New York. My mom may not have wanted me to leave, but she felt better knowing I was with my older brother Lamar.

All of my brothers and I were a part of this ministry when it was in Chicago. It started off as a Bible study in the home of the minister. He led a deliverance ministry. He taught us so much about the Bible and God. He taught us about Black Hebrews and our origins. We did a lot of studying. I dedicated myself to God and doing God's work at eight years old. This minister also led a lot of revivals, so we'd travel with him around Chicago and even to other cities later. It was fun being around other young people, and I felt called by God to be of service.

I wanted to continue in service to God; I didn't think I needed school. I already knew I was called to do God's work, so when this minister decided to pick up and move to New York to do God's work, I wanted to join in on the movement. By this time, my older brothers (Ray and Robert) had stopped attending our Bible studies and traveling with the minister, but Lamar and I were all in and followed the ministry to New York. In fact, Lamar went before I did, and I followed him to New York. He leads this ministry in New York to this day.

One of the reasons I wanted to go—in addition to doing God's work—was to get away from Chicago. At that time, gangs were bad. It seemed like every day gang members were chasing me and trying to recruit me to join one gang or another. I literally would have to run home to avoid them. Luckily, I was young and fast.

In New York, the teens in this ministry stayed in three kitchenette apartments in Spanish Harlem. About five of us stayed in one room. We had pullout sofas. We each got a job too. At sixteen, I worked as a teller at Citibank. I told them I was eighteen—I had the papers to prove it thanks to my mother. After work, the youth in the ministry attended revivals with the minister. We thought of the ministry as our main job. When we had to go out of town, we just picked up and went and forgot about work. I remember telling my manager at Citibank that I had to go home to Chicago for a funeral. I said my mom died or an aunt had died, but really I was going with the ministry to a revival. I think my job even sent flowers to my home in Chicago to acknowledge my relatives' deaths, but I was not there. I was doing the work of God with my brother and others. We sang, led praise and worship, and evangelized to all who would listen. We were a nondenominational and very charismatic ministry.

People were drawn to this ministry. The team lived in three units in the apartment building, and we raised money for a church that the minister later opened in New York in Harlem. It was a small storefront church, but we had big hearts and a lot of passion. We'd go down to Time Square, which always has a crowd of people, and solicit money for the church. We told people what we were doing, and they freely donated. That's how we were able to open a church.

We raised a lot of money. In the church, I played the conga and drums. My brother sang. My brother was more of a teacher, and I was more of a preacher.

My time in New York forced me to grow up quickly. I held many jobs before the age of twenty because I often needed to quit to go to a revival away from New York. My father's work ethic made me a good employee. I didn't have trouble finding my next job.

While I loved New York and working for the ministry, I made my way back to Chicago around age twenty-two. The minister asked me to go back. He wanted to start a church there and recruited me to help.

CHAPTER 2

Moved Back to Chicago

As I was coming of age, I preached God's love and believed in God's love, but now looking back over my life, I realize that I didn't love myself. Even though the greatest commandment (see Matthew 22:37–40) instructs us to love God with our entire heart, mind, and soul and to love our neighbor as ourselves, I don't think I knew what it meant to love myself.

I probably didn't know it as a young man or didn't have the words to explain it, but I always had a problem with my skin color. I am dark skinned, a rich mahogany color—not that I would have used such an exquisite adjective to describe myself in my youth. No, instead, back when I was much younger, some would have described my color as midnight, dark, or sambo. I didn't like being Black, nor did I like being dark skinned. I wasn't the only one. My sisters used skin bleaching cream to try to garner a lighter hue. They too thought lighter skin would make them look better. Now juxtapose all of this Black hatred with my father who spewed hatred toward the White man. He had grown up under the oppression of White people, and his only response to them was hate. I was caught in the middle—hearing how awful White people were yet not loving myself as a Black male either.

All of these emotions were hidden as I tried my best to follow God. The ministry in New York had been a wonderful experience for this West-Side-of-Chicago youth. I had gained my wings and flown away from my mother and father. I had honed my preaching skills and enjoyed passionately leading worship and Bible studies. What was next?

The pastor I served under in Chicago and New York wanted to open a church in Chicago, and he needed help. He asked me to leave New York and return to Chicago when I was twenty-two. I did. I didn't go back to my mother and father's home. I lived with the pastor at his home in Chicago. I also found other jobs in Chicago at banks. And when I wasn't at work, I worked for the ministry. I joined others and went out and asked for donations. I felt like I was doing my mission: helping the church and sharing the way of salvation with others.

For most of those years—from my teens to about age twenty-five—I felt fulfilled. I felt as if I was on the right path, but one thing began to really bother me. It became such an issue that I questioned the ministry I was serving.

Becoming a Young Man
Courtship and Marriage

As a young man, I had urges, and I was just tired of being alone. Our pastor taught that if God had called you as a single person, then you should remain single. You should do as Paul said in 1 Corinthians 7:8 and dedicate your life to the work of the Lord.

I understood this scripture, but I was also yearning for a companion. Did I really want to live the rest of my life as a single man? No, I needed someone in my life. I didn't think my pastor would approve of my wanting to turn in my single card and gain a wife, so after a lot of thinking and praying and pondering, I decided to leave the ministry I had dedicated my life to as a teen. I just disagreed with his theological understanding about singleness and marriage. And I wanted to be married.

Around the same time I was grappling with my theological understanding of marriage, I met the woman who would become my wife. I do believe once you're open to something, things start to happen. And right there, in a revival on the South Side of Chicago—

while I was busily doing the Lord's work with our ministry—I laid eyes on a beautiful young woman. I remember her great smile the most. It was hard to focus on the revival; shoot, if the preacher would have given me a test right after he preached, I probably wouldn't have been able to repeat anything he had said. My eyes were fixed on the pretty lady in the pew toward the back.

This young lady had light skin and long hair. She sat in the middle of the church and looked like she enjoyed the service. She looked just like the image of beauty I had conjured in my mind. I was drawn to her. I watched her from the other side of the church and wondered, *Who is that lady?*

I wanted to meet this pretty woman, but naturally my shyness didn't help me here. I just took glimpses of the beautiful young woman at the church every chance I could during the revivals. I was still the same young child who hid under the table when my sister's pretty light-skinned friends came over. I was not used to talking to girls. She was attractive, which didn't help me as I was extremely shy and didn't think very highly of myself.

Thankfully, our revival lasted all week, and I looked forward to each night just to take a look at her. Toward the end of the revival, I got the courage to speak to her. She was carrying a camera, and I used that to break the ice.

"Do you know how to use that thing?" I asked pointing to the camera.

She gave me one of those smiles I had seen just by staring at her throughout service. From there, it was easier to talk to her. We exchanged numbers, and that night I went home happier than I had felt in a long time. The revival had been great, but meeting this beauty had sparked something I had never felt before inside of me.

The young beauty seemed interested in me, which made me very happy. Turns out we had some things in common. We believed in church and trying to live according to the Word. She made me smile and laugh too, something I hadn't done much of in my twenty-something years. I had been so committed to ministry at a young age I hadn't experienced joy and the carefree life of youth. I had been a boy in a suit and tie at fifteen dedicated to sharing God's Word. I was serious about God and ministry; now I had this giddy, happy feeling. This was all new for me. Being with Nita, the pretty young woman, made me feel happy. Seeing her and thinking about her brought me a lighter, joyful feeling. I hadn't experienced this feeling in life. I knew it must be love.

However, as I look back—because hindsight is truly twenty-twenty—I realize I was not only young in age, I was young and naive about love and marriage. I really didn't have a good model of how a man was supposed to treat a woman. While my dad taught me to work hard, he didn't teach me how a man should treat his wife. I observed him abusing my mother; I knew he had another family outside of the one he had with us. I just didn't have a picture of how a family man should be. Nor did I know how to truly get to know the woman I intended to marry.

Nevertheless, I entered into a marriage with Nita after we dated for less than a year. Now when I say we dated, let me be clear: She lived with her pastor and his family with a very strict, holy, and sanctified background. And I was committed to honoring God and not doing anything to break my covenant with God. We didn't go on dates without a chaperone. When I visited her at her godparents' home, I sat on the opposite side of the room than she did. They were always in the room with us. We managed to sneak in a few unsupervised dates. I'd meet her downtown where we both worked, and we'd get a little kiss in—but nothing else. We were virgins. And I was happy to marry her. I wanted someone in my life. I thought this was how things should be.

I did have to deal with my pastor who disagreed with me getting married. He thought I should stay dedicated to the ministry; I felt I could do both. I could be a married man and committed to serving God. So since I was living at the pastor's home, when I decided to get serious with Nita and think about marriage, I left his home. I moved into a YMCA on the South Side of the city. It was the first place where I lived by myself. I stayed there until Nita and I tied the knot. I didn't go back to my parents' home because I was ashamed. I hadn't lived with them since I left for New York at fifteen. I hadn't visited them much since I had been back either. I thought it was best to just stay at the Y and focus on the new life I'd build with my new soon-to-be bride, Nita.

Nita and I were married on a hot summer day in June 1979 at God's House of Prayer. I was looking forward to a lifetime of happiness. I just didn't realize I needed to be happy and complete by myself before I tried to merge my life with my wife's—and I would discover this later.

We were both excited about our life together, and we found out shortly after our wedding night that Nita was pregnant. We were going to have our first child and become a family of three—just months after joining together. We didn't see any issues with starting our family so quickly. We felt blessed by God and continued full speed ahead to try to find our happily ever after in marriage and life.

Another Hero Emerged
Robert Earl Williams

When I moved back to Chicago, my older brother Robert Earl emerged as another hero that followed in my dad's footstep of being a hard worker. The strength of our family was working hard. So now I have two heroes: my dad and my big brother. Robert even worked with dad and some of his brothers and sisters at Dayton Electric. Robert, after finishing high school, enrolled in the military, the US Marines. I call him, even today, big Earl; he served four years. Robert got through basic training with no problems because of his work ethic as a hard worker.

After basic training, Robert and his high-school sweetheart, Linda, got married in the front room of our west-side apartment on Congress Parkway. As it stands today, Robert and Linda have been married for fifty years and still in love. It takes hard work to stay married for fifty years. Returning to the military, his unit were assigned to serve in Vietnam for one year. Robert finished his four years tour of service to his country and returned home to his family.

Some time after returning home, Robert began to make plans of entering the work force and made plans of what field of work would be best for him. After talking with his wife, he decided to start school to be a registered nurse. After finishing his RN program and becoming a nurse and finding a job, he didn't stop there. Big Earl, while serving as a nurse during the day, started law school at night. He attended ITT Law School in Chicago, Illinois. Later, Robert and his family left Chicago and moved to the East Coast and to New Jersey. He finished his law degree at Rutgers University. In addition, he became licensed in three states—New Jersey, Pennsylvania, and Delaware—where he investigated complaints against hospitals and nursing homes until he retired. Watching Robert's life and family gave me the audacity to persevere through life and work hard at whatever came. The same work ethic has been passed along to my children, grandchildren—and hopefully—to my great grandchildren as well.

CHAPTER 3

First Child and Church of God in Christ Affiliation

Our first months of marriage were good. Naturally, it took some time to get adjusted to living together, but we did. And we had the excitement of our first child looming in the air. We thought we were living the life; this felt like the way things were supposed to be—marriage, baby, life.

We did have that transition adding our first child to the mix, Charles E. Williams II. We were members of God's House of Prayer Church of God in Christ, where we got married. I joined the church right after we got married and worked in the church. I continued in ministry, and we both were committed to the church. I joined the staff of ministers there at God's House of Prayer, where Pastor Jessie Ewing was pastor. Nita and I served there for about two years.

We knew no church was perfect, but when the pastor at the church got Nita's best friend pregnant—even though he was married to another woman—we just couldn't stay at the church. We visited several others churches, while seeking God, for a new church home. While we were visiting Saint Peter Church of God in Christ on 127th Street, just for fellowship, Pastor James Sims was preaching that night. After church while leaving the parking lot, I ran into another car. Pastor Sims helped me and my family get things sorted out with the other driver; this is how I met Pastor Sims. The next week, we visited his church on 147th Street in Harvey, Illinois. This was the beginning of a wonderful relationship. Nita and I, after some weeks, joined Pastor Sims's church.

Commit to Serving the Church, Then Second Child

Even as I worked to be a good husband and father, after about a year, we got involved at Outreach Church of God in Christ. I continued to do everything possible at the church. It's what I was accustomed to doing at my former church, giving my all to the service of God. After some time, I became the church's secretary as well as financial secretary. I sent out a lot of correspondence for the church including members' giving statements. I kept all of the records and financial statements for the church. I was the person the pastor relied on for anything legal. Now I wasn't a lawyer, but I knew where to look to find out what we needed for our deeds, taxes—anything. I got things done. If that wasn't enough, I also helped the guys clean up the church on Saturdays. We made sure our church was clean, and we were proud to keep it that way. After cleaning the church on Saturdays, I also worked with our homeless ministry. We provided food and clothes, and I and other ministers gave messages to encourage those who came to keep going and to trust in God. On Sundays, Nita and I both taught Sunday school before service. At times, I picked up members in the church van. Then I sang in the choir, where I served as president, for a while. I was one of the first to arrive at the church and always one of the last to leave. My wife and son drove together in her car because I was always at the church much earlier and much later than anyone else. And I also took a lot of church work home. If I didn't get something done at the church, like the paperwork, I would bring it home with me.

You see, as a young child, I missed out on the nurturing of my mother. I didn't like my skin color, and I didn't feel good about myself. I didn't have a model of how a man should be except to be a hard worker. No one had ever told me "great job" or that they were even proud of me. My parents were just too busy trying to survive. So when the folks at the church gave me attention, thanked me, and looked to me for help, I loved that feeling. It made me feel valued, welcomed, loved, and good. My void was filled by the praise I earned from working hard and doing good works. No one could have told me this was wrong or that my motives weren't good. I thought this was all good, necessary work; and I was happy to do it and happy to be wanted and needed—so much so I neglected my wife and didn't grow into the man I needed to be.

I didn't cheat or run around—at least not with another woman. You see, I think I made "good" works my true desire; I was always at the church doing "good" works. I did any and everything the church we attended needed. I now realize I was addicted to the affirmation of others. I wanted to hear "good job," and I did whatever needed to be done to hear those words. After some time, my marriage suffered because of this. I felt I wasn't giving my wife enough time.

Several years later, Nita became pregnant again with our second child, Jeremi. Now this pregnancy was a lot different than she had with Charles a few years earlier. Nita suffered from high blood pressure while pregnant and had difficulty delivering Jeremi. Both of them almost died, but thankfully they made it through. Understandably after surviving Jeremi's birth, my wife decided that she never wanted to go through that ordeal again. Because of the difficulties of her second pregnancy, she decided she would not have any more children. She got her tubes tied. I was happy. We had our two boys, and I had my wife. We had always wanted a girl, but I also understood my wife's need to take care of herself. I didn't want her to go through what she had been through in delivering Jeremi. So we went on as a family of three. Thank God we made it through and lived what I thought was a happy life with our sons.

As I said earlier, I never saw doing too much for the church as a problem. Nita and I were both Christians and had been in the church since we were young. Wasn't this what I was supposed to be doing? I was committed to serving God and gave it my all, never considering I was sacrificing my family or myself. I didn't think there was anything wrong with giving my all. Yes, I enjoyed the accolades, but I didn't know that could become addictive or even problematic. I had dedicated my life to God at eight years old; I really didn't know anything else.

Second Child and Second Job

Now with a family of my own, I of course continued to work hard—as my father had instilled in me since my birth. When my wife and I started out, our money was very tight. Adding our son to the mix early on in our marriage made money even tighter. We were a young family, and we had expenses. But, as a hardworking man, I wasn't going to let our financial situation sink us. I took a part-time job because I wasn't making enough at my full-time job at Seaway Furniture. My wife also worked; she had a job downtown at Chicago Title and Trust. Neither of us made very much. I made less than $100 a week. With rent, utilities, and our growing sons, we barely had enough to put food on the table.

As a man, I felt it was my duty to find more money for our household. To make ends meet—well as much as possible—I started cleaning carpets for Carpet One. The way the job worked was I'd get 50 percent of whatever I made. So if I took a job cleaning a building for $300, I would make $150. This side job helped us make ends meet; and I was able to do it after work, on weekends, and in between all of the work I did at the church.

With the additional income and us being very careful with what we spent, my wife and I were able to move our little family into a small home in Blue Island, just south of Chicago. Thankfully, we got a mortgage that was less than the rent we were paying for an apartment. It was a nice home, and we made it ours. I was convinced more than ever: hard work could pay off—just as my father had showed me.

Around the time I settled into raising our two sons, I got a feeling that I wasn't doing all I could for myself or for my family to have a good life. I wasn't feeling like a man, even though I was providing for my family as my father had instilled through working two jobs. I didn't feel worthy. I kept thinking of myself as a failure. Here I was almost thirty years old with two boys who would look up to me, I hoped, and I had less than one-half credit of high school. I was still a high school dropout. Yes, I worked hard and provided for my family, but there was something missing. My church work couldn't fill the void, and neither could my wife. If anything, being a father made me want to do better. I needed my boys to see more. I just didn't feel good about myself. Perhaps pursuing an education would help build my self-esteem.

Back to School at Age Thirty to Earn GED and BA Degree

At thirty, I took a big leap and decided to add school on my list of things to do. I kept my full-time job and my part-time job because I didn't want my family to suffer financially. And I wouldn't dare leave any of the church work undone. (I didn't think I could as I took my calling seriously.) Since I had only completed a half of credit my freshman year, I needed a GED. I took prep courses, quite a few, to help me pass the test. I had to take the GED test at least four times before I could pass it. But when I did, it was one of the proudest moments of my life. I felt like I had set out to accomplish something and did it. For the first time in a long time, I felt good about myself.

That feeling of accomplishment is addictive. So after getting my GED, I decided to pursue my bachelor's degree. When I took the entrance exam for college, my scores were very low. I couldn't take the college level courses right away, I had to take years of non-accredited courses. But I was determined. I took this class by class and kept my focus. It was very difficult, but I got through. There are some classes, like algebra, I had to take more than once to pass. I took algebra four times. It took me that long to be able to average a C in the class. That C was like an A to me. I knew how hard I had worked for it.

I went to four different colleges to get college credits. I attended the University of Illinois at Chicago, East West University, Moraine Valley Community College, and Harold Washington College. I was determined. Once I had enough credits, I got into Governor's State University in University Park, just south of Chicago, to complete my junior and senior years of college and get my degree. At the time, the college only accepted you when you had about sixty credit hours. It was a junior and senior college. Thankfully, the program recognized life experience as valuable. I received twenty-five credits for the experience I had accumulated throughout life—living basically on my own since fifteen, traveling the country, doing ministry, and working at several different banks and other jobs. Those twenty-five credits put me closer to my goal. But even with those credits, it took me a total of seven years to get my BA degree, overall. In my last semester, I took six courses (while working) just to finish my degree. I passed all of those classes and was able to graduate with a concentration in computer science and business and management.

School didn't come easy to me; remember, the most I had done was one-half of a credit of gym in high school. I had trouble taking notes because I didn't spell well. I had to think a little harder to try to spell words while listening to the instructor. Eventually, I learned to listen very carefully because I couldn't rely on my notes.

I learned a neat trick during this process. If I asked the teacher a question, especially an open ended question—just enough to let him or her know I was paying attention—then the professor would explain the concept completely again. My questions would get my professors to talking more, elaborating on the subject and giving me another chance to hear what I needed to know—without my notes.

Figuring out what was going on with my courses was just part of the battle for me in school. I was older than most students. I encountered teasing and even racism.

I was called old man and treated like one. Whenever we had to form a group to study or for a class project, no one wanted to work with me. I was the old man with the notes that were hard to read if readable at all. These younger students didn't recognize my life wisdom like the college did. To them, I was a dumb old man, and they didn't want anything to do with me. I admit my notes were horrible. I had a tough time understanding, and my spelling was atrocious. I also couldn't type well. Spell-check didn't help me much because you have to start the word off right. I didn't know a lot of words, and neither did I know how to begin to spell them. I typed my papers with two fingers. When I attended one school to work on my beginning college credits, I was even put on academic probation. Many just didn't think I could do the work.

Somehow even with my learning issues, I found time to do all I needed to do while in school. Both of my sons were into little league baseball, and I made all of their games. I even coached one of the teams. And I was able to branch out from my part-time job and take on clients for myself. I started my own carpet cleaning company: Charles and Sons Carpet and Upholstery Cleaning. I took my sons to help me out in the business. I got even more clients because people really liked seeing my young boys working with me. They admired that I was teaching my sons how to work early. To this day, both of them are hard workers. They've followed in my footsteps as well as my father's footsteps. They know the value of working hard.

Meet Major Thomas Lewis, Employed by the Salvation Army, Family Income Increased

Charles and Sons had a client, Major Thomas Lewis, in Elmhurst, a western suburb of Chicago. I'd clean the carpets in his home often, and I got to know him well. By this time, I was no longer working full-time at the furniture store and had gotten a job as a computer operator at BJ Fasteners. Major Lewis knew of my work, and he knew of my character. He liked me and offered to help me get a job at the Salvation Army. He gave me the name of the director of data processing, Major Norman Nonnweiler, at the Salvation Army. I called him every other day. I wanted a better job and had heard so many good things about the Salvation Army. I thought it would be nice to work there. The director told me he would let me know when a position became available, and he did. I was offered a job as a computer operator at the Salvation Army, and my salary doubled.

My wife also got another job making more money. She moved to AT&T. It seemed as if things were looking up for us. We moved to a bigger home, a very nice home in a suburb of Chicago. At the time, a new subdivision was being built, and we were able to choose what we wanted in our home. We watched it being built. In some ways, it was like watching our dreams come true, one brick by one brick. Our hard work had paid off, and we'd get to move our boys into a lovely home in a quiet, family-oriented suburb.

Just like all marriages, my wife and I had issues or little problems, but I didn't think we were going through anything time couldn't fix. I knew I was focused on school and work and church. In fact, my wife wanted to go back to school also. I asked her to wait until I was finished with my degree, and I would give her the time and space to pursue her goals. I thought she was okay with this, and I continued to focus on getting my bachelor's degree. It took me about seven years to go from earning my GED to getting my bachelor's degree.

And back at home, I thought things were fine. My wife continued to work and care for our family well while I pursued my educational goals. My wife was supportive. She helped me with my papers because she was a much better writer than I was. Somehow I missed the signs that my wife was not happy. She played the part of wife and mother well, in my opinion. But deep down, she was not happy. She felt like she had not had the time or the opportunity to discover who she was. I think in some ways she resented that I was getting to follow my dreams while she held down the house. Even though I thought the family was both of our dreams, I missed how angry she had become.

We married in our twenties and started a family soon after. She had been a dedicated mother and wife, and now she wanted to find out who she truly was. I was confused. We had arguments and resolved them rather quickly, in my mind. We worried about the normal things couples do, but we kept going. I was moments away from obtaining one of my goals. I had worked hard to get to this place, and we had built our dream house together. Shortly, with me finished with school, I told Nita she could be free to go back to school and get a degree too. I just wanted her to wait until I was done.

She listened, I thought. She continued to help me reach my goal and celebrated with me as I graduated with my bachelor's from Governors State University. Sometime later at the Salvation Army, I got promoted to programmer.

Employed at Coca-Cola

Two years later, I got hired to work in the data processing department at one of the largest companies in the world—Coca-Cola. This was a dream come true. I, the young boy who dropped out of high school with just a half of credit at fifteen, was now a full-time employee at a global company. I was thankful, grateful, and appreciative of all God had given us. And my family, including Nita, had stood by my side and supported my goals.

In my first day of work, I drove in to Coca-Cola in Niles, Illinois, a northern suburb of Chicago. I set up in my beautiful office and took it all in. When my wife called, I thought I would get the chance to describe my office and the view. But I didn't. She called and was upset because she had not attained her goals in life. We had a conversation about her going back to school.

I told her it takes time. "You can't go to school like a teenager. You have a young family, and your education has to be planned."

I couldn't believe what I was hearing. She was not happy. She questioned our marriage. I had gained everything I had worked so hard for and dreamed about, but now my wife didn't want to be a part of it anymore. This news startled me and took me totally by surprise. I was totally blindsided.

I asked her to go to counseling. I realized she was very angry about a lot of things in our marriage. This took a toll on my wife. My lack of attention for her had also taken a toll. I was too focused on my goals thinking it would help us all, but she wanted more. She wanted my attention. And as I reflected over our relationship many years later, I also realized I didn't get a chance to know my wife before we were married. Our courtship was pretty short. And I was inexperienced, so I didn't know what I should be looking for. We both had some tough unresolved issues, and those things built up and caused hidden issues in our marriage.

CHAPTER 4

Adoption of Third Child, Nita
Back to School, Starts Business

I must mention one of the beautiful moments of our marriage. It's still funny how life can be filled with trauma, even if I didn't realize it at the time, and still birth beauty. While my wife had decided to stop having children after the serious complications she encountered when delivering Jeremi, our desire for a little girl lingered. I had never thought seriously about adoption; but when my youngest son was four, my wife and I opened our home and, most importantly, our hearts to a girl child. We adopted our daughter when she was just two months old. After talking about our desire for another child, my wife and I went to a Christian adoption agency. We completed lots of paperwork and endured through a background check. All we went through was worth it when we saw the first picture of our daughter. We gave her the name a coworker came up with; his name was Jerry. He said, "Use part of your name and your wife's name." We chose Charnita.

Nita enrolled in a fashion design school downtown Chicago plus she started sewing on the side to help make ends meet. In addition, she made outfits and sold them in the flea market. Her business's name, Charnita's Fashion, was a combination of our names: Charles and Nita. The naming of our daughter as her business would seem like another symbol of our togetherness and teamwork, in my mind. For a while, we lived as a happy couple with three beautiful children. I just never saw what was really behind my wife's smile and both of our willingness to do what we needed to do for our family.

Blindsided by Wife's Unhappiness, Marriage Separation, and Fired from Coca-Cola

I was a mess. First, I was blindsided by my wife's unhappiness. I had spent more than seven years pursuing my GED and college degree. I had to focus on school and learning and being an older student in a traditional class setting. I had to take classes several times to get a passing grade. I was working and fathering and trying to save money to care for the family. In between all of this, I just missed my wife's unhappiness. Looking back, I could see that she was very angry about a lot of things. It wasn't just my inattentiveness; she had been through a lot in life and had not dealt with those feelings. I thought we could get through those things. After all, I was a provider, a hard worker, and a good father. I loved her. Wasn't that enough?

Three years later, her baby sister came to town on an educational scholarship, and she moved in with us. Nita saw her younger sister moving ahead with her education and a brighter future; this added heat to the fire. Sometime later, my wife decided to go through with a separation. She moved downtown Chicago with her sister. I was lost. How could this happen? Hadn't we finally gotten to the point we had worked for—the big house in the suburbs, three beautiful and happy children, and my degree? I literally went to work at my good new job and cried every day. I had a nice office with a picture window, and I spent lots of time just staring out of the window. I couldn't pull myself together to concentrate on the work. Nita and I tried counseling, but things were not going well. I literally walked out of counseling sessions several times. My wife had so much embedded anger, and she accused me of many things that hurt me. She clearly had a point, but I thought I was doing what was best for my family. I thought I was supposed to work hard for my family and for my God. What more did she expect? Want? Apparently she needed more, and I didn't know it. I didn't give it to her. She had already made up her mind—even when we went to counseling. She was done with us. She was leaving and wanted a divorce.

Even my father who didn't interfere in my personal life much saw what was happening.

He told me, "That woman is done with you, boy." He said he could look on her face and see that she was done. And she was.

One day, my boss at Coca-Cola came into my office and told me directly, "Charles, Coca-Cola has invested a lot of money in you. We are paying you quite a bit of money to do this job."

I explained to him what was going on in my life, but I knew my time with the company would come to an end soon.

Another day, I asked him outright: "When are you guys going to fire me?"

"On Friday," he replied.

Returned to Salvation Army, Divorce Happens, Holding on for Reconciling, Starts to Meet Other Females

It was Monday. I had one week to prepare to leave the office.

I called Major Lewis, my client and boss, who helped me out at the Salvation Army.

"Major, I have a problem," I told him. "My wife left me and I can't do this job. Would you see if I can come back to the Salvation Army?"

"Yes, Charles. You can come back. Your office is still here, and we haven't hired anyone. Come back."

The work ethic my father had instilled in me was still helping me. I was able to do my old job without thinking. I needed that during this time.

As for the divorce, my wife and I decided to ask the judge for split custody. By this time, she had left Chicago and moved to Atlanta and was staying with a friend. She wanted us both to raise the children, me in Illinois and her in Georgia. The judge granted us our wish, but he later told me he would have given me full custody if I had requested it. He saw me as a stable father. I still had the home, and my ex-wife was not really settled like I was. We worked out where the kids would stay with me during the school year and would spend the summer with her in Atlanta.

At one point, we decided to have the youngest children, Jeremi and Charnita, go to school in Atlanta and stay with Nita. I kept the oldest, Charles, with me in Illinois. That didn't work out as well as we expected.

One day Jeremi, in Atlanta, asked his principal if he could call his father. When I picked up the phone, my son said, "I want to live with you, Dad. I want to be with you and my brother."

Nita didn't want Jeremi to move with me, but she saw how much he was suffering. So she let him come live with me. I had the boys during the school year, and then I had my daughter for the summer while the boys were with their mom. My daughter learned to fly by herself at an early age. The airline workers knew her. I'd fly Charnita back to Atlanta early so she could get a chance to have a few weeks with her brothers. It was tough. It was really hard on all of us but especially the children.

Deep down, I still had hopes of reconciling with my wife. With just one word from her, I would have left my life in Illinois and all the hard work I had put into getting what I wanted to move to Atlanta and be with my wife. I would have given up twenty years of hard work just to still be married. I was a mess and only kept it together for the kids.

One day, Nita saw me in my sad state and asked me, "Are you going to die for me?" She saw how I was wasting away, unable to pull myself together. She continued, "I don't want you; why are you willing to die for me?"

As much as those words hurt me, they woke me up. I had to follow her questions with my own questions.

I dug deep and asked myself, *Why are you walking with your head down? You look all defeated.*

I had a female friend who sat me down and gave me a real warning. She told me—from a woman's perspective—I shouldn't quit my job and give up everything to move into Nita's world. I wouldn't be respected. I wouldn't be happy, nor would I be able to make her happy.

So the only thing for me to do was to deal with myself. For the first time since my few months in my little apartment in the YMCA, I was alone. I had to learn to live alone even as I tried to raise my children and co-parent with Nita.

When I sought counsel from my pastor, he said, "Boy, you need to shop around before you marry somebody."

He advised me to date different women and get to know them. I also realized that I hadn't dated. Nita had been the only woman I showed any interest in.

So the newly divorced minister-since-his-teen-years went out into the world to date—to find himself and find another mate. What a mess. To say I was naive doesn't adequately describe me or the situations. I was always a giver, and I think some women could see that. They took advantage of me quickly. I bought lots of gifts and paid many bills just to gain approval. I liked being needed, and some people can sniff that out right away and use that to their advantage. I can't blame them fully, however. I wanted someone to approve of me, and I was willing to do whatever it took to gain the approval. But I was the one with the problem. I needed to work on me.

I realized this after a particularly painful conversation I overheard. I was into this woman, and we had been dating for a few months. If she told me she needed something, I would do everything in my power to give it to her. I thought that was my job. Then one day, I heard her talking to her sister on the phone. She didn't know I had showed up at her apartment a little earlier than normal.

She laughed and then said, "Girl, this man is a fool. He buys me everything. He is so stupid."

I was hurt, but I was also glad I knew exactly how she felt. I was strong enough not to give her another dime. I moved on and met other people.

During this time, I also picked up a hobby that helped me meet women. I started skating. I'd go to the skating rink every time one opens. A lot of people around my age would hang out at the skating rink. It was fun. I happened to befriend three sisters, and they made it their mission to look out for me. They'd prescreen the women I skated with, telling me, "Don't skate with that one" or "She's not up to any good, so skip her." They were very protective of me and only let me skate with people they "approved of."

They also invited me to parties and were just as committed to watching out for me there as they were at the skating rink. They didn't let me dance with anyone they thought was "fast" or who wouldn't be nice to me. These sisters were truly godsent. They kept me away from a lot of trouble.

I also had a friend name Pam. She and I would skate often. She was very nice and kind. One day at the rink, she told me she wanted to introduce me to her best friend.

"She talks about church all the time just like you do," Pam told me.

But months passed by and I still hadn't met Pam's friend.

I finally got the courage to ask Pam, "When are you going to introduce me to your friend?"

She gave me her friend's number and I called her.

That call turned out to be one of the best moves I'd ever made.

CHARLES WILLIAMS

CHAPTER 5

Divorce as Death

But before I share the blessing I found as a divorcee, let me share some of the lessons of perseverance I learned through the horrific pain of divorce. As a minister—a young man raised in the church since a young boy—following God and following God's Word was all I knew; it's all I wanted to do. I had committed myself to ministry and wanted to please God. Divorce was never a thought for me. I believed God's Word—when you join together, you are joined together. No matter what. But as life would teach me, not everything was in my control.

My divorce left me spiritually dry. I didn't question God, but I questioned everything about my situation. I had done just as my father had taught me through words and deeds—I had worked hard. I took side jobs to provide for my family. I had even turned my part-time carpet cleaning job into a business for myself. I taught my sons how to work hard. I got extra business because people loved seeing me bring my boys on the job, making them fill the buckets and help me clean carpets. I supported my wife during both of her pregnancies and had happily welcomed our daughter into our lives. I had dealt with my self-esteem issues, so I thought, and pursued my education. I went from a half of credit in PE to a GED to remedial college courses to an actual degree. And once I graduated, I encouraged my wife's desire to go to school. We were living the dream, in my mind. How did this happen? On the day I started a job as a computer programmer at a solid company like Coca-Cola, I faced divorce.

While my ex-wife picked up and moved away, I was left in Illinois in our big house—the one we watched built from the ground up together, the one we brought our three kids to and tried to give the good life, the dream. I was alone and sick and tired and confused and just dry. Divorce really is like a slow death. Not only was my marriage done, I felt as if I was dying and being buried. And to not realize something was this wrong really blindsided me. Nita's leaving hit me hard. I didn't have time to brace for it either. I really felt like it was my death and burial.

I didn't feel like going back to my old church—too many memories. It was where we had worshipped together. The beautiful people at the church just loved me so much, and they looked like they had so much pity for me. I didn't want to face them. I didn't want to see the sadness reflected in their eyes and in their words of concern. I just didn't want to deal with all of that.

I really decided to visit other churches when I heard a few well-meaning sisters at Outreach Church say, "Doesn't Brother Williams look bad?"

They were right, but I didn't need to hear that. And I didn't need to see the sadness in their faces. I already felt bad enough.

Visited other Churches, Heard Powerful Messages, Victory before Midnight, Broken Focus, Victor through Jesus, Thou God Seeth Me, Armor of God, Decisions That Could Alter One Destiny, and God Is My Shepherd

So I visited other churches I had heard about in my many years of ministry around Chicago and suburbs. I had been in church all of my life so I knew a lot of places to go. While I was mad with God and questioning what was going on in my life, I didn't know any other place to turn except to God and the church. I tried to sneak in the back and sit silently with my pain. I didn't really want to talk to anyone. I just needed to hear from God.

As I look back, each and every one of the sermons I heard during this time spoke directly to me. God heard my cry. I needed to know that God was still right by my side.

I still remember many of those sermons—from many different churches that I slipped into and sat quietly, praying and anticipating God's Word.

One was titled "Victory before Midnight," and it came from Acts 16:25–34 where Paul and Silas prayed at midnight when they were locked away in jail. The preacher said midnight is the darkest hour and it is just before the break of day. I felt like it was midnight in my life, so the message of the daybreak approaching gave me hope. I needed the new day; I needed the light as I sat in the darkest hour of my life.

Another message I heard during my dark days was titled "Broken Focus." This message was preached by Pastor James Sims as I stood in the back of the church. The word *broken* described exactly how I felt inside. I felt as if my world had been broken. Who I was and what I lived for had been separated, and now I was left to figure things out. In this message, which really was about when our focus is broken, from Matthew 14:23–33, the preacher talked about a familiar scripture where Jesus was walking on the water and Peter wanted to come to see Him. Peter was able to walk on water like Jesus when his eyes were fixed on Jesus. Peter was able to do the impossible when he stayed focused. But when he took his eyes off Jesus and let them gaze around him and on his situation, he began to sink. When our focus is broken, we are in danger of sinking and being destroyed. In that message, I heard that I needed to stop focusing on my hurt and pain and brokenness—my current and real situation—but to instead focus on my God. I heard this message at just the right time in the back of a church. It was time for me to stop grieving what I had lost and think more about God. My pain didn't immediately dissipate, and my circumstances didn't change. But I returned my attention to God and all He was still doing in my life. I changed my focus from my broken life to all I still had.

I also recall a message entitled "Victory through Jesus" from 1 John 5:1–5 which also tied into the earlier message, although I was at a different church. This message reminded me that Jesus is the Word of God, and I needed to stay focused on what the Word was saying to me. I have victory through God. Regardless of how I felt, regardless of the dreams that were dashed and regardless of the pain that seemed to come out of nowhere to pierce my soul, I knew I had victory. That victory didn't look like I had planned. But I believed God and believed God's Word, so hearing this message encouraged my soul to stay focused on God. I was encouraged to see victory even in my broken marriage and my broken life. I'd been walking with God too long to start doubting now.

My cloud began to lift, and I still visited different churches, now excited to hear what the Lord was going to reveal to me that week. I heard messages from Romans 8:37 that reminded me I was more than a conqueror. I needed to put aside my defeated spirit. I was acting defeated, not like a conqueror. This message gave me courage. The messages God was sending my way through the preached word were life-changing. God heard my cry and sent me messages.

One particular message from Genesis 16 really resonated with me—and it still does even to this day. It was Hagar's story. Hagar had been treated terribly by Sarah, Abraham's wife. You probably know the story about how Sarah commanded Abraham to sleep with Hagar to produce an heir. But when Hagar got pregnant, Sarah turned on her and made life a living hell for Hagar. Because of her pain, Hagar ran away. She thought it might be better to be homeless than to live under such oppression and abuse.

This text showed me that people close to you can hurt you. I wasn't alone. People hurt people. First, I had been hurt by my church and had to leave it with my wife. Then I had been hurt by my now ex-wife. She had run away from me and our marriage, leaving me broken and hurt.

But the message in Genesis 16 is that God saw Hagar. Pregnant and alone, Hagar heard from God. And that's when she said, "You are the God who sees me... I have now seen the one who sees me."

In her distress, in her dire situation, and in her brokenness, God sent an angel to speak to her; and the angel let her know that God heard her misery. The angel even told her what to name her son and told her who he would become. In the midst of all of this, God saw her. In the midst of all I was going through, God saw me. I felt hopeless and alone like Hagar, but this message was like a spring of water in my soul. God was sending me more and more messages to remind me that although I was divorced, I was not alone. Although I felt misery, God knew all about me. God was still in the very midst of my situation. That sermon was preached by Richard D. Henton, and he called it "Thou God Seeth Me." To this day, I recall that message and have used it to get over anger, and I've shared it as a word of comfort for others grappling with hurt and pain especially from loved ones. No matter how you may feel, God sees you. I can still cry now when I think about how this sermon ministered to me in the very midst of my most painful experience.

Other sermons included putting on the whole armor of God, which came from Ephesians 6. I heard about decisions that can alter our destiny, which dealt with Joseph in Genesis and his decision not to sleep with Potiphar's wife. If he had not made the right decision, it would have altered his destiny. But even when we make the wrong decisions—like David did with Bathsheba in 2 Samuel—we can repent and come back to God. These bad decisions can affect our family and the people close to us, but God can give us another chance.

Psalm 23 also ministered to me as it reminded me that God is my shepherd and is here through all of my troubles. He comforts me through still waters and in my valleys. The still waters remind me of places of comfort. With all I was going through, God's presence was with me. Somehow I would get through this.

When I think about how I got over during this painful time, I know those sermons were specially crafted for me and my situation. Somehow, almighty and omnipotent God placed me in those churches on just the right Sunday to hear those messages. You couldn't convince me that those sermons were not crafted for me. You couldn't convince me that God was not leading and directing my course even in the darkest hour of my life. Realizing this gave me hope. Realizing this drew me closer to God and deepened my faith. Truly this trial was strengthening my faith and shaping me in ways I could never have foreseen. I was living out what James 1 says to consider it pure joy when you face trials—they truly do produce perseverance. And that perseverance is what we need to be mature, complete, and whole.

CHAPTER 6

Meeting Carol, My Resurrection, Courtship, Combining Children, Premarriage Counseling, Confronting Our Baggage from the Past Marriages of Carol and Me, Early Marriage Problems after Some Years

My divorce was a horrible, slow death and burial. But the Christian story doesn't end with the suffering and death of Jesus. What gives us hope is the resurrection—when Jesus defeated death and rose with all power in his hand. I had heard that message over and over since about age eight. I had preached that message many times. I believe that message. And somehow God arranged things where I'd live that message, even after many years of dedicated ministry. Going through my divorce nearly killed me, but somehow and some way, God saw fit to give me another chapter in my story. While it seemed like life with my divorce and remarriage, it was really a story of death, burial, and resurrection. I call her Carol.

During my recovery process after my divorce, I took up skating as a way to learn to enjoy myself. I really didn't know how to just have fun—not working one of my jobs, studying for my degree, taking care of my family, or doing something at the church.

Skating became my outlet, and it was a good way to meet people. As I said earlier, I found three sisters who looked out for me. They didn't let me hang out with women they thought would be no good for me. They often stopped me when they saw me about to approach a woman—even just to skate around the rink. Every time the rink was open and I wasn't working, I'd go skating. I didn't want to be idle, and I wanted to meet others.

Then there was Pam Snow. She was very nice and kind. We skated together a lot at the rink. Pam told me she wanted to introduce me to her girlfriend because we both talked about church all of the time (it was all I knew to talk about).

Pam kept telling me she'd introduce me to her friend. But her friend wasn't a skater, so she wasn't at the rink with us.

I asked her after several months, "When are you going to introduce me to your friend?"

Pam finally gave me her friend's number, and I called her. We went out on a blind date. That was Carol. We got married about a year and a half after that first blind date.

Now with Carol, I did things differently than during my first courtship. We took a full year to get to know each other. When we got serious and started talking about marriage, we agreed to go to premarital counseling. I felt like we needed to have professional guidance to think through the possibilities and prepare ourselves to spend our lives together. It's something I wish I had done the first time around.

Carol had a daughter from a previous marriage and, of course, I had my kids. She eventually introduced me to her daughter and I introduced her to my children. We brought our kids out with us and let them get to know each other. We went bowling, out to dinner, roller skating, and to church as a couple and with our children. Carol's daughter, Megan, was sixteen and still in high school. My oldest son, Charles Jr. whom we called Chuck, was fifteen. Jeremi was eleven, and Charnita was seven. Our children got along pretty well given the new circumstances for them. At the time, Charnita was living full-time in Atlanta with Nita while the boys were in Chicago with me. Nita and I would meet up midway in Kentucky to exchange children. I even took Carol to Kentucky with us so she could meet Nita. At the time, Nita was good with things and seemed okay with the new woman in my life.

Carol and I talked about our expectations and wishes before marriage. We agreed that we didn't want to have any more children; we were both in our early forties. I was working at the Salvation Army data processing department and trying to make ends meet on my one salary after having been used to a two-income household.

I had to overcome some financial challenges at that time. I bought a cheaper car when I ended up having trouble paying for the one I had and made some other changes.

I had some tough decisions to make, and I didn't want to enter my new marriage with financial issues. I moved closer to work and didn't have to pay for the tolls. I lived close enough to my job to ride my bike or even walk to work. I rented out the house Nita and I had built from the ground up.

My move, however, also meant my boys had to go to a new school. I lived in Mount Prospect, Northwest suburbs of Chicago, and the school was all White. Chuck was about sixteen at the time. This was a tough change for him. He eventually went to stay with his mother in Atlanta. My youngest son, Jeremi, stayed with me and continued at the new school. He did well there.

After prayer and counseling and some sacrifices, Carol and I got married in 1997. We moved into the home I had left in the suburbs. One of the most sensitive situations I had to work on was Carol's mistrust issues. She had been in an abusive marriage and could not trust her ex-husband. He had been an addict and had cheated on her. She stayed in her marriage for twenty years and had been through a lot. She was an enabler to him and was hoping he would change. But what really happened was more disappointment which led to her mistrusting him, and I thought it would trickle down to me.

I needed to understand how this situation impacted her and handle it with care. She talked about her situation, and she knew it weighed on her and could impact our relationship. I was a man of integrity, and I was used to taking care of my home. I always told Carol what I was doing with our money—showing her the bills I was paying, trying to help her see that I was not her ex-husband. I was not going to abuse my power as her husband and protector. She could trust me.

It wasn't easy. I had to pull back sometimes and share more other times. I loved this woman, and I wanted her to feel comfortable and trust me. Understanding her baggage was a part of loving her. Adjusting my ways was a part of being a better husband. I had to remind myself of this often. I think I paid for the sins of her husband, but I loved her and wanted to prove to her that she could trust me. We visited our counselor often to help us get through our early years of marriage.

I had my set of issues too. I caught myself backsliding—or trying to—when I was single. I did things I had never experienced before. I went to clubs (and ordered diet coke). I told myself I wanted to date "sinner" women, not the good church girls; my three sisters had friends they wanted me to date. But I never fit into this lifestyle. I still remember trying to talk with women amidst the loud music at the club.

"Huh, what'd you say?" was all I could ask them. I couldn't hear a thing with that music. They often laughed at me because we couldn't talk.

I went on a cruise with some friends; it ended up being twelve of us. They'd stay out all night, but I couldn't hang. I'd go to my room around 9:00 p.m., and they'd ask, "What's wrong with him?"

I just wasn't used to this lifestyle. It wasn't me.

I tried dancing too. A friend named Vanessa tried to teach me how to dance.

"Move your hips, move your hands and your head."

She couldn't understand how I couldn't dance. But I was a true church boy at my core. I had thought dancing was wrong, and I had never tried it. Now at forty, I couldn't do it.

I eventually learned how to step with Carol. She had been a party girl and knew how to dance.

With Carol, I had to be careful not to go into my shell and be afraid of getting hurt again. Whenever something reminded me of my ex-wife or something she had said or done, I retreated. The pain and hurt from our divorce still hurt me. I had baggage just like Carol, and I had to deal with it. If I wanted to love again, be married again, I had to overcome some of the things that had hurt me. We both really had to learn how to trust again.

Serving with the Salvation Army, First Appointment at the Freedom Center as Chaplain, and Finished First Master's in Pastoral Counseling

After Carol and I married, the Salvation Army, who likes when couples work together, offered her a position. We decided not to join either one of our churches but to become a part of the Salvation Army.

I was appointed at Harbor Light at a Salvation Army, which was a substance abuse center for men and women. I was the chaplain at the center. I learned a lot about the street life here. Even in my forties, I hadn't done a lot nor been exposed to the lifestyle some of the men and women we worked with had endured. I had never done drugs, smoked, or used alcohol; so I was not certain I belonged at a substance abuse center. I wasn't sure I could help anyone there.

At the center, I handled the Sunday night service and offered counseling to anyone who needed to talk.

When the Salvation Army asked Carol to work for them, she wasn't very receptive to the idea. She was working at Bank of America at the time and making good money. She didn't want to give up her job. Instead of encouraging her to join me at Salvation Army, I prayed. I asked God to make a way for her to leave her job if it was His will for her to join me at Salvation Army.

And eventually, she resigned from her job at the bank. That's the door that opened for her to come to the Salvation Army. We had a wonderful time serving together at Harbor Light. Carol was a volunteer for a time. We connected with the clients even though they came from different walks of life. We met doctors, lawyers, and politicians who needed to utilize Harbor Light's services. A lot of judges were in the program. They had done some crime and were sentenced to work release programs at Harbor Light. Even pastors who hadn't paid taxes were sentenced to our program.

Carol and I prayed together and studied together, which helped build our marriage. We had offices next to each other at Harbor Light, and we really were never out of each other's sight. Serving with the Salvation Army was a blessing that strengthened our marriage.

While I was never shy about preaching, Carol didn't always feel comfortable delivering God's Word to others. She had self-esteem issues after her years of being in an abusive relationship. I knew I needed to help build her confidence, so I did encourage her to preach and share with others. I was there with her when she needed more confidence. She really was very good and had a great presence. When she developed her confidence, she became very impactful.

Carol and I have now been married for twenty-two years. Looking back, I can see that we had some very good times and some very rough times. She had to deal with her trust issues. I had to deal with my sometimes regrets for not living a "normal" life. I hadn't sowed any wild oats, and the enemy made me think I had missed out on some things. I started looking over the fence wondering if there were things I should do. I can laugh about that time in my marriage now, but at the time, I was in a battle wondering if I should do some of those things I hadn't done. I was tempted to jump over that fence, but I didn't.

I had even gotten to a point where I told Carol I didn't want to be married anymore. I wanted to go out into the world and have fun. She talked to her old pastor, Bishop Arthur Brazier; and he counseled her to separate herself from me, not to leave me but to sleep in another room to give me space. During that time, Carol prayed mightily for me. I heard her in the next room praying, reading scripture, and singing gospel songs.

Hearing my wife call my name out in prayer and try to rebuke the devil on my behalf got to me. It wasn't what she said to me but what she said to God that got me to reconsider wanting to try out a different lifestyle. I wanted her. I wanted her love and devotion. I wanted to work this marriage out. I turned my back on the temptations facing me, some in the form of clients who tried to persuade me to come to their side. Many of these clients had been trained to seduce and were quite good at it. But God's power kept me and brought me back to my right mind. I've always had the fear of God in me, and during this trying time, God used my wife to bring me back to my senses. I thank God I didn't do anything that would permanently harm me, my wife, or our marriage. God heard her prayers.

God did not leave me even when I was in the midst of a battle of my mind and will. When God loves you, God chases you. I'm a friend of God, and He did not leave me. As David says in Psalm 23, goodness and mercy followed me. God's goodness and mercy chased me down and brought me back.

One other particular incident stands out when I think about the rough times of my marriage. One time, Carol got upset and ran up to me. Carol had been conditioned to be tough and not take a lot of stuff after all she had endured.

She got in my face and yelled, "Where have you been!"

I had been gone most of the day on a Saturday, and she thought I was out doing something wrong. We were together most of the time, but she didn't know where I was. I'm not a physical person, and I didn't want her to hit me. In her previous marriage, she was attacked a lot. She had learned to fight with her words, and those words hurt me badly.

This made my temper flare too. I had never been a fighter. When I saw my father abuse my mother, I vowed never to hit a woman. And I hadn't. So despite my anger, I told Carol to "get out of my face. Whatever you do, get out of my face."

Thankfully, she backed up, and we both calmed down and eventually were able to talk about the situation.

Throughout our marriage, I've learned what can challenge me. I know her insecurities can crop up and cause her to lash out. I'm thankful that these outbursts haven't led to violence. Through these twenty-two years of marriage, I've learned how to be quiet when she rises up like this. I know I can't change my wife. I need to love her as she is. And I now know that I'd rather have peace at home than to be right. There are times I just have to let some things go. I'd just rather be at peace.

CHAPTER 7

Salvation Army Appointments of Carol and I Started and Finished Second Master's, MDiv, Started My DMin Program, and Finished It in Omaha, Nebraska, Appointment Became Dr. Williams

Working at the Salvation Army with Carol was good for our marriage even when it presented challenges. We were together all the time and were able to grow together personally and professionally. As I said earlier, Carol was a gifted teacher, but she needed to build her confidence. It was my pleasure to help her grow in this area and to see how her ministry impacted others.

We were each other's biggest supporters in ministry, and that was refreshing. Ministry was my life, and I felt honored to be able to share it with Carol.

The Salvation Army proved to be a blessing to us too. Even while we were sharing and giving to others through our calling, God has a way of pouring back into our lives. We were blessed through ministry. Giving really can be a blessing to the giver as well as the receiver. I was connected to the Army for twenty years as an employee and twenty-two as an officer in many different appointments and even different states. Each one presented its own rewards as well as challenges.

The Salvation Army had many policies in place that helped us as employees. First they wanted Carol and me as a married couple to work together, and they supported us in whatever way they could to get us together. After Carol resigned from her job, she joined with me in ministry. The Salvation Army also wanted us to live in their quarters, so they purchased our home, which allowed us to be free from our mortgage and live where we were assigned.

The Salvation Army offered us the opportunity to move several times and work at various sites. After Harbor Light, we moved to Brained Corps on the South Side of Chicago and led the church.

One of the marks of transformation I had been desiring to see throughout my ministry was evident in seven families at this church. When we arrived, these couples were living together. They had families but had not committed before God in marriage. I taught them biblical concepts and counseled them all. I didn't judge them, but I did share what God's Word said. Before we left that appointment, all seven of those couples decided to join in marriage. They committed to each other and to raising their families together.

We had an exciting Bible study during our appointment there too. People couldn't wait to get to the midweek service. We were, as Paul says, ones who plant the seed. God made them flourish and grow. And that's what preachers do: deliver the mail and share the message. God provides the growth.

It was a blessing how we got to the Salvation Army training college because of the people we were serving at this appointment. Carol and I were envoys, so that meant we were basically contract employees for the Army. We were the pastors at this small church, and we had a great congregation. There were some people there we encouraged to attend the Salvation Army training college. We wanted them to become official officers because we recognized their leadership abilities.

We were urging these three members to attend the Army's training college, and they turned around and said to us, "Why are you all telling us to go to the school and you've never been?"

They were right. They made a very valid point. Carol and I prayed and talked about it and decided to go. We were not too old to learn more. I had been to school as an older student before; surely I could do it again. So again, those we were giving to actually gave to us. Carol and I became cadets. We gave up the pastorate and moved to the North Side of Chicago to attend the training college. I was blessed to receive credit for my many years in ministry, and I finished in one year although the program was two years. I stayed on campus an additional year until Carol finished. After I completed my officer training, I also went to McCormick Theological Seminary and earned a master of divinity. I had previously received a master of pastoral counseling in 2001 from Olivet Nazarene University.

Another great part about the Army is their policy of enrolling into training college debt-free. They think it is important for you to not have ties to debt. In some cases, they even help you get debt-free before you enroll. Carol and I were pleased to give up our debt in exchange for learning more about ministry. For those with young children, the Army sends their children to private school, and they have a day care on campus to care for those who are not school-age.

Because I only had to do one year (of a two-year program because of my experience), I did get some pushback from other cadets. Here I was, an older man among many other students, and I was promoted quickly. I was given credit for my work experience and was in the same class as cadets who had already put in a full year of training.

While Carol finished up her training, I was appointed to the Red Shield Center in Chicago, and I was still able to live at the training college. The Army sold several of their church buildings and combined congregations at the Red Shield Center. They even built a beautiful facility and asked those congregations to move there as one.

The Red Shield Center proved to be a great appointment for Carol and me. We served there for three years. The facility was great and allowed us to share with the community in many ways. We had a running and walking track in our gym and a commercial kitchen where we were able to have cooking classes. We offered sewing classes as well as computer classes for seniors and GED programs, which was very special to me since I had worked very hard to get my GED. We had family counseling, and we rented the state-of-the-art facility out to other businesses. Even the City of Chicago had an office in that building. It was in the heart of the Englewood Community and was able to have a big impact on the residents. Some were however connected with gangs, and there was a lot of violence in the neighborhood. You could hear gunshots often and many people were killed in those streets. I dealt with fear during this appointment, and I prayed for God to move us. Also, we started a thanksgiving community dinner served by the Chesses Cake Factory. It stared out serving 150 people, and today the totals are about 800 people being served.

From the Red Shield Center, we were appointed to the training college into administration. I really loved the Salvation Army and the work they did and are still doing. I wanted to be a part of the training college. I worked in administration. During my three years there, teaching was part of our assignment. Major Fleeman, the principal, assigned me to teach several courses to the cadets. I was eager to put all I had learned into instruction and training for others. I taught pastoral care, which I loved. Then I was asked to teach a class on racism. While it was important for cadets to explore their issues around race, I didn't want to be the one to teach it. I knew some wouldn't handle it well and would be offended. I don't think people are naturally racist, but they are often shaped by their experiences and what they see and have been exposed to. I didn't think the White cadets would take kindly to a Black man teaching a class on racism. Up until the first day of the class, I told Major Fleeman of my apprehension of teaching such a class. In the class, I had a few Hispanic students and one Black student.

I started off the class by telling them, "You're going to get offended. You will offend me. You are going to get mad. I apologize now because I know what we cover in this class will hit sensitive areas."

To this day, that was the best class I've ever experienced. We unpacked what the cadets' families taught them about race through actions and comments. The N-word came up, and we explored what it really meant and why it was offensive to Black people.

There were tears, there were breakthroughs, and they were all necessary.

I told the cadets, "You're training to be a pastor, and you can't have racism in you when you're preaching the gospel. This is the place to get it out of you."

We ended with many apologizing for their part in racism and for what their families had taught them. Even the tough guys who didn't want to talk broke down. I saw transformation through this class. One student brought his Confederate flag and talked about what it meant to him and his family. These exchanges were challenging to me to say the least. Yet it became a powerful class. I saw people repent; I saw people cry about what was said about Black people. We discovered that we were much better than that as Christians; we unpacked why we thought the way we did, who had influenced us, etc. I also shared with the cadets how my father had hated White people and how that impacted me, hearing those words growing up. Together, most of my students and even I repented for our thoughts and actions. We agreed to continue to do the hard work of figuring out our contributions to racism and moving forward. Even today, I still reflect positively about that class. It was truly meant for me to teach the class I never wanted to teach.

I see it as a moment where I was able to see exactly what God was able to do. I hope and pray those lessons have continued to live with those cadets as they serve people around the world. I hope I inspired them to not talk down to people and to make sure they check their own biases before standing before people. I hope they are still breaking down the barriers and walls. Multicultural communications was a class that changed me, and I know others. It marked one of the most beautiful moments of my three and a half years at the training college on staff.

While I was teaching, Carol worked as the health officer. If someone at the college (or their families) got sick, they would see Carol before going to the doctor. She also worked with the food service in charge of feeding the cadets and staff and planning menus and events. She eventually moved to teaching health classes and starting a wellness program.

After our servicing at the training college, we were appointed to Kansas City, which was a hard appointment. Our marriage and ministry were tested greatly in Kansas City. I was stressed and burned out. Both Carol and I questioned if we wanted to continue in ministry.

This was a very needy community. I wanted to preach the Word because I'm very serious about God's Word. I think knowing it intimately is transformative.

But I learned I needed a different approach depending on the needs of the people. In this community, we had a high number of people with mental illnesses; many were homeless and sat in the back of the church because they knew we served food after church. We never turned people away even when they were at service for ten minutes. The Army attracts a lot of needy people. Word gets around when people are giving food and shelter out. And of course, many genuinely needed the help. Others knew that this was a good place to get stuff. At Christmas time at the church in Kansas City, we had a huge toy drive. We gave away many new and nice toys and people knew this. Some came simply for what they could get. This bothered me. I was a preacher. I wanted to give the gift of the Word and help people meet Christ and become transformed. Seeing hundreds of people pour in for toys bothered my spirit when these same people were not being transformed or impacted by God's Word. Some just want to use the church. Some even professed to be Christians, and I suspect they said this just to reap the benefits we were giving away at the church. The fruits of their lives did not show what I believed. I tried my best. I counseled people. I preached and prayed. I even visited many in their homes and tried to help them. But the fact that the same people would show up with the same needs every week, month, or year clearly meant we weren't changing their situations. They still had rent due, electricity bills to pay, etc. I thought: *What is it that we are doing that these people are not getting better? How are the same people still having the same issues after so much time?*

Observing this situation prompted me to work with the Army's program, Pathway to Hope. I had this idea right about the time the Army introduced it. It was designed to help move people from needing help to being self-sufficient. The family that owned Hallmark gave the Salvation Army millions of dollars to develop this program, and I was fully behind it. I wanted to stop giving out fish and start teaching people how to fish. I believed most people had it in them to care for themselves and their families. I wanted to stop giving handouts and truly give people a helping hand so they could care for themselves and truly live in this life and find their God-given purpose.

I wanted to help the Army ask the right questions when training the needy: What happened that got you in this situation? What could we do to help you move away from this situation? I wanted to see more success in our programs. I didn't want people just to show up, confess the Lord, and turn away and keep living the same way they were. I wanted to see change.

But even with these difficulties, I did see victories at this appointment. We had a feeding program and served 100 to 150 people each day. It was a blessing for us to help meet the needs of the people. I also met a woman at this appointment, and she went on to attend the training college for the Salvation Army. Her name is Patricia Williams, and she is serving now in Milwaukee, Wisconsin. Because of her name, many people think she's my sister. She is just evidence of the fruit we saw even in the midst of a difficult appointment.

The type of work we did in Kansas City, combined with the type of heart I had, can be tough. I got overburdened and felt like I needed to pull away from the pulpit. I told Salvation Army that I'd rather be moved to another appointment. I didn't want to do the ministry in the church as pastor anymore. I thought I'd rather be a chaplain elsewhere.

So off to Omaha, Nebraska, Carol and I went. There I was appointed as a citywide chaplain for all of the Army's twenty-six in-house social services programs. I remember serving at the senior resident home, Booth Manor, the most. Prior to my coming, there was a chaplain there the people really connected to. She was a White woman, and she served the mostly White community. There were only a few Black people living in the home. When I started as the chaplain, I immediately knew this would be a challenge. I didn't feel welcomed at all. In fact, many of the residents refused to talk with me. They asked where the other chaplain was. I wanted to do my job. I was supposed to be at this home at least twice a week leading devotions, singing, praying with residents, etc. I wanted to help meet their spiritual needs.

When I visited other nursing homes, I always wore my uniform—a very recognizable uniform in this area. But one day when I walked into this home to visit a sick resident, there was a group of all White women just staring at me, wondering why I was there—in uniform, mind you.

"Can we help you?" one said tersely.

I promptly answered and said the name of the sick elderly resident I was there to visit. These women did not believe I was the chaplain.

After checking with the front desk, I guess these women were convinced, but I was still escorted to the woman's room. That made me feel some kind of way. But as soon as I got to the room, the sick woman sat up straight and said with glee, "Oh, my chaplain is here." She was an elderly White woman.

You could have heard a pin drop as those women stared in astonishment.

This type of encounter made it very challenging for me to minister in Omaha. But I kept doing my work, and eventually the people began to love me and look forward to my visits.

One of the few Black residents even refused to talk with me. JR was an ex-military person, and I kept trying to talk to him. I persisted. He had cancer and was dying. When they moved him to the veteran's hospital in Nebraska, about three hours away, he asked me to come visit him and walk with him through the valley of the shadow of death. I had gotten through to him and provided comfort for him. He requested to see me before he died. It was my honor to sit with him during his final hours of life. The day after my visit, he died.

I think how I got through to JR made others want to open up to me too. They saw my compassion, my persistence, and my commitment to serving. In the end, this appointment turned out to be a blessing.

My appointment in Omaha was the greatest work I had to date. I was able to meet people from all walks of life. It started off rough, and I persevered through the racism, stereotyping, and even the rejection. I still did my job as a Salvation Army officer and served people.

While working as a chaplain, I decided to get certified. I had done lots of ministry work with people, and I thought it was important to have the certification. I knew I was called by God, but I thought it would help others understand this if I was certified. I learned a lot through school and certificate programs and believed in education. I wanted to add the credentials to my experience. I wanted to be even better equipped with chaplain skills. The training helped me with ministry to mentally ill and dying people. This was not always things you'd learn in the church. I walked away with lots of tools to help me with people in nursing homes and other situations. I was certified through the chaplain ministry association. I learned most of the stuff through online classes, but we also met regionally and attended the annual conference each year. I became a clinical chaplain and then a board-certified chaplain. I'm still a member of that association now.

Our last appointment with the Army was at Harbor Light in Detroit; like in Chicago, Harbor Light is a substance abuse center. This became our last appointment when my wife was diagnosed with Hodgkin's Lymphoma Cancer. We went on medical leave at first, but then Salvation Army allowed us to retire six months later in 2019—about one year earlier than planned—to focus on Carol's healing.

CHAPTER 8

Enduring Racism, Stereotyping, Racial Inequality, and Racial Profiling
Journey of Sickness
God's Healing

Throughout my journey as an employee and during ministry, since age fifteen, I have endured much when it comes to racial injustice. I endured racism, stereotyping, injustice, inequality, profiling, and working on an unlevel playing field. In this chapter, I will share many of my experiences. All my encounters were with individuals and systemic racism.

I experienced not being trained the same as a White employee. When I asked questions, I was told to read the manual. But this White employee was given hands-on training by a White staff. This is an example of an unlevel playing field. It's one reason why people of color many times are left behind and overlooked.

During ministry, other white ministers and staffer would avoid me on purpose. They would talk to my wife to not have to talk with me. I was overlooked on purpose. I felt disrespected as a Black man. This an example of racial profiling about Black men to keep them down.

While living in a ministry quarters in Evergreen Park, Illinois, one of the best-looking homes in the community, we had an alarm go off 2:00 a.m. in the morning. My first thought was to protect my family. I picked up a baseball bat and started to walk through our home. Then, two White policemen arrived. All the policemen in Evergreen Park knew who we were, and that I was a Black man because Carol and me were on the primetime news three days that week. The news was about the home our ministry purchased for us as a ministry quarter. So when the policemen arrived, I met them at the front door. First comment was, "Show me your ID?" My wife was sitting on the stairs, calm. They had guns on me. They looked at my wife and asked, "Ma'am, are you all right?" She responded saying, "He is my husband." I felt so bad and didn't want to live there anymore. This is a case of stereotyping and racial profiling.

Another experience was in Omaha, Nebraska. I was assigned to serve as chaplain at a senior home. The senior home was 90 percent White. I replaced an older White female chaplain. I wasn't received very well by most of the White residents. I took this as a testing of my faith. I knew it was going to be a difficult task. But I was ready for the task. Part of my role was to visit all residents in their homes, hospitals, lobby, and even sit with them at lunchtime. Also, I did devotions twice weekly. Plus, part of a new book club. Before finishing my appointment there, they all were in love with me; some even cried at my farewell. I overcame the racial stereotyping and profiling by God's love.

In Chicago, I was a volunteer chaplain, working with an older White female. I wasn't received very well. Her being uncomfortable made residents feel the same way. Some time went by, and everyone were able to see what was going on, including the staff. God always have a ram in the bush. At a major staff meeting concerning other some different matters, the CEO asked, "Did everyone meet our volunteer chaplain?" She began to share some remarks about me that she had heard from other staff and residents. It took another White woman to speak well of me, to open doors for me with the staff White chaplain. Again, racial profiling and stereotyping of a Black male.

In another assignment as pastor and counselor, I felt me and my wife wasn't invited to certain tables, where we can be part of the conversation for a change. We prayed about it and then wrote a letter to the top management and our direct boss. We went to a regional conference where the leader preached about welcoming others to the table; it's time for a change. We brought it up when we got back in town, and it wasn't good because some thought we were rocking the boat. Rocking the boat happens when change comes. This was a case of inequality, not thinking we were able and not good enough to be around the table.

My next experience was getting into a college to start my master program. I had worked hard to earn my BA liberal arts from Governor State University. It took me eight years to earn my GED and then my BA. I enrolled into a higher education school, Olivet Nazarene University. I got accepted. They didn't think I could do the work. I felt I was being racial profiled because I had no high school education, just my GED. I was put off academic probation for two years. Well, out of the twelve classes, I got ten As and two Bs.

In addition, when I had finished those two degrees, I went on to earn another master, my MDiv from McCormick Seminary in Chicago. I felt as Black man I need to be double qualified; it's the reason I wanted two masters. Some years later, I decided I want to earn a doctor's degree. So I started my search for the right school. I found Luther Rice College and Seminary in Georgia. I forwarded all my transcripts and filled out my application. I wasn't accepted. This felt like racial profiling all over again. I need only a BA and one master to get accepted into any DMin program. Well, I had earned BA, MPC, master in counseling, plus MDiv more than enough. God had another ram in the bush. I made a call back to McCormick to a White professor I knew. He made a call to Luther Rice College and Seminar and asked why I wasn't accepted. I got a call ten minutes later. "You're accepted." I don't know what was said on my behalf, but it took another White male to speak on my behalf to a White staff. Another case of racial profiling and injustice.

Being part of a sterling committee for young pastors, I was the only African American around the planning table. The dominant culture always took control of the meeting. When I would speak, they were not conscious of my concerns. It happened so much; I stop voicing my thoughts. It's just what they wanted for me—to be silent. The chairperson saw what was happening; he asked me to share my thoughts even for ten or fifteen minutes. I made comments about three young pastors I thought were accepted into the program before they were ready. They didn't think I was right. All three were dismissed from the program before they could complete. It turned out they weren't ready as I said. This is a case of profiling, not thinking I was smart enough to see and make that call.

In Omaha, Nebraska, I was the city chaplain for all social services programs for our organization. They had twenty-eight in-house programs, the largest in the nation. You name it, they had it. I got a call one day that one of our seniors was sick and want a visit at her nursing home. I rushed right over. When I entered the doors in this small white upper-class community. There were at least twenty White women in a board room meeting. Every one of them stopped what they were doing; their lips dropped and turned around in their chairs, looking at me, like a ghost had enter the building. The clerk at the front looked at me as though I was in the wrong place. I said, "I'm here to see one of your clients." I gave them her name, and she called reinforcements to the desk to help. At least five other staffers came running to the front desk. I had all my minister clothing on and name tags from where I was from. All the staffers walked with me to the room. God had another ram in the bush. As I entered the room, where this small white woman was lying, when she saw my face, she sit up and smiled and said, "My chaplain is here. Thank God." You could hear a pin drop, and smiles came on all the White faces.

Lastly, I earned my doctorate in ministry with a focus in pastoral care. Many in the organization had a problem addressing me as Dr. Williams. It was always captain, chaplain, brother, reverend, Envoy, and Williams. Why could it be Captain, Dr. Williams? I'm not tripping on doctor. I worked hard to earned my degrees.

If I had to sum up my life story in one word, it would surely be *perseverance*. I've learned the hard way what that word means. I know what it means to persevere throughout life. But if I had to change my life's story, I don't think I would. The things I encountered in life made me build my spiritual and emotional muscles so I could persevere; those things are as much a part of me as the great things that happened in my life. In fact, because of what I have had to overcome and go through, I can call my life great. I have learned to lean and depend on God for everything. I've learned and tried to share with others that God will use the rough things in our lives to bring us to a new place. My health challenges have also been a part of that story of perseverance.

My family has historically had bad kidneys. My grandmother died on a dialysis machine in California. Then I have an aunt on my father's side who also died because of her kidney function. She didn't want dialysis, so she met an early death. A cousin on my father's side was also on dialysis.

Then it was my mother. She was a dialysis patient for about ten years. And my father was on dialysis for fifteen years. He eventually received a kidney transplant, but died the next day from a massive heart attack.

My brother Lamar, who still lives in New York working with the ministry we joined in our teens, has received a kidney transplant. And my brother who lives in Memphis, Montes Foots, his son, my nephew, lost a kidney and received a transplant. So it is probably an understatement to say my family has been plagued with bad kidneys.

And I have been too. About fifteen years ago, I lost one of my kidneys and had to go on dialysis for nearly three years. At the time, I was a cadet and later appointed as pastor at Red Shield Center. I had graduated from the Salvation Army school of ministry and was still working in my calling. I didn't skip a beat even though I underwent dialysis treatment four times a day, every day. I chose to have the treatment at home so I could continue working and not have to take the time to go into a center. But this means I had to make sure everything around me was sanitized. I had fluid delivered to my home, and I needed my wife to help me pick them up. We had some delivered to my office too because I was determined to keep working while I went through this. We even took a cruise and had to have the fluid sent to the ship so I could continue treatment while vacationing. This went on for three years. During this period, I had several infections, and I was diagnosed with congestive heart failure.

Dialysis is used to remove the waste out of your body, mainly because your kidneys can't do that job. So when you are on a dialysis machine, it filters out your blood, taking away any waste and extra fluid you might have in your blood. By filtering the blood, it cleans it and then returns it to the body. With dialysis at home, I used a tube from my stomach to connect to the fluid. I had to make sure no air got in the tube during this process, which also can cause infections which can lead to death.

During a trip to South Carolina, I thought I had met my end. I had so much fluid buildup in my body, my organs felt like they were beginning to shut down. My wife was with me on this trip. The doctors in South Carolina consulted with my doctors in Chicago, and they told them what to do and what not to do for me. I thought this would be the end, but thank God it wasn't.

Even coming to near death in South Carolina, I didn't stop. I truly believed what I preached, and the deliverance ministry I grew up in had a lasting impression on me. I believe that God is a healer, and I believed God would heal my kidney or provide me with a new one before it was too late. And even if he didn't, as the Hebrew boys said in Daniel 3:17–18, I believed He was able. Going through such a health crisis feels like its own fiery furnace, but I kept pressing and believing.

At the same time as believing in God's ability so strongly, I also struggled with the grief of losing my kidney. This was a vital part of my body, and it was gone. High blood pressure runs in my family, and that can damage your kidneys, which happened to me. Anxiety and diabetes also runs in my family. These diseases can impact the kidneys also. I had kept good control of my blood pressure until my thirties when I was diagnosed with diabetes, which also impacts the vital organs. My kidneys were damaged little by little throughout my life because of the high blood pressure, anxiety, and diabetes.

Even with my strong faith, I questioned God. I asked, *Why me?* I told God my résumé as if He didn't know it. *I have been there for people all of my life. I've seen You do miracles for people. Why not me? Why am I struggling?*

Through my questions, it seemed like my God was silent. But somehow, I still found the strength to preach during this trial.

I was at Red Shield Corps in Chicago. I saw the ministry blossom even while I suffered. My skin turned even darker as a result of the dialysis. I was already really dark and had struggled with my skin tone for years. I didn't look good. Every morning, it was a struggle for me to get up and keep going. But somehow, I did. I still believed in God and His power. Even when I had doubts, I prayed and believed. My faith still existed even in my times of questioning God.

One particular low moment for me during this illness was when my wife went to a women's camp. I remember it clearly because it was a Thursday night, and she wasn't due back until later that weekend. The camp was in an area with no cell phone reception, and I was all alone. I felt horrible—physically and emotionally. I just wanted to give up, and I felt sorry for myself. I couldn't even reach my wife. That weekend was one of the toughest times in my life. As I look back on it, that was my midnight moment—you know the time when things are the darkest but daybreak is right around the corner.

That Thursday night I got up and went to Outreach Church, Pastor Sims called me up and shared a prophetic word.

He said, "Young man, come up here. God has a word for you. God said in two weeks, rain and blessings of God will fall in your life."

Every day I was looking for God's blessings and the rain to fall in my life. I trusted in God's Word.

Two weeks later on a Thursday night, I went to a church prayer and praise meeting with the youth. Eric Himes was the youth speaker for that night. I still remember he preached from Psalm 139.

He said, as if he was speaking to me alone, "God knows everything about you, going in and coming out."

That night, God brought the answer, which gave me strength. I had been angry about my health condition. God sent the answer through the Word of God. It was two hours before midnight, and the two weeks would have been over, in which pastor Sims spoke, concerning my health. He said, "In two weeks, God will send his healing powers." Our young people were there with me and my wife; they left encouraged.

My silent God really wasn't silent at all. God used others to bring words of comfort to me at the right time. The prayer and praise meeting were over just before midnight, and we got in the van around 9:45 p.m. My wife was driving, and I was in the passenger seat next to her with the youth in the back of the van. I felt my phone vibrate, and I answered, wondering why I was getting a call at this hour.

"This is Charles Williams. Who's calling?"

The voice on the other line said, "It's Rush [a hospital in Chicago]. We got a kidney for you. How soon can you get to the hospital?"

Knowing the distance from where we were, I replied, "We can get there in thirty to forty-five minutes."

My wife drove straight to the hospital; she didn't even take the youth home. They came to the hospital and prayed with me.

They told me, "You've preached and said God was going to come through. It's our time to minister to you."

Even in the midst of that breakthrough—which was two weeks after that prophecy—the devil tried to enter my mind and play tricks on me.

A voice inside of me kept saying, *You're going to die. I'm going to kill you just like I killed your father and all those in your family who died without a transplant.*

It was truly a battle for my mind. I got myself together and told the devil, *I'm going to live and not die*, right there in the hospital pre-op room before my transplant.

Eventually, someone from our church came to the hospital and drove the youth back home in the van. We had called their parents and explained what was happening. My surgery was scheduled for the morning.

When the team showed up to take me to surgery, the doctor said, "You could die from this surgery."

I looked at the doctor and said, "Not today, Doc. I'm not dying. Let's get on with it."

That was the last thing I recall saying before I went to sleep and they started my surgery.

After the transplant, I was in intensive care (the ICU) for recovery. My pulse was close to 200, and it was my nurse's first day in the unit by herself. She had seven patients that day. My blood sugar was also extremely low. It was as if the devil was saying, *I got you now.*

But I still told the devil, *I'm going to live and not die.*

I told myself to just relax and take deep breaths. The nurse eventually tended to me, and my pressure started to decrease.

I stayed in the hospital for five to six days after the transplant. That was thirteen years ago. My kidney is still working just fine. I've had no problems, and I thank God for it all.

When we moved for the appointment in Kansas City, I had to transfer doctors. My doctor there introduced me to a woman who had been living with her transplanted kidney for thirty-three years. That gave me encouragement to keep going.

God answered my prayer for a kidney in His time, and I am forever grateful. I don't take it for granted that I got that call from Rush around 9:45 p.m. after our prayer and praise meeting. I don't take it for granted that, that was just before midnight. It's true. That was the darkest time of night. It was pitch black outside, and it felt uncertain and unsafe. But God moves just in time, and God moved just in time in my situation. There was truly victory before midnight.

While I believe most of my kidney issues were just hereditary, I do some things to keep myself healthy. I keep my diabetes under control with diet and exercise. I'm conscientious of my stress and what I eat. I share my testimony with people all of the time in the midst of health battles, and they are always blessed by it. What God did for me, He can surely do for others.

Joy truly does come in the morning—as my midnight call demonstrated. As soon as I got that new kidney, my skin color returned to its normal coloring. The blood started running properly through my body—the blood that didn't have toxins and impurities in it. My kidney was able to produce clean blood on its own.

I still have to get my blood tested every two months to make sure my organs are functioning properly. I see my doctor once a year.

At one appointment, my doctor said, "You really take good care of yourself."

I don't play. I ask questions and stretch even my doctors. I stay on top of what I need to do. I eat on time, and I take my meds at the same time each day. God has given me another chance through my health battles, and I want to do my part to maintain good health. It's my way of saying thank you to God.

CHAPTER 9

Conclusion

In conclusion, everyone in my family was a hard worker, and it's the example that they set forward through many generations. My father, mom, grandfather, grandmother, great-grandfather, and great-grandmother were all hard workers and didn't get the chance to attend school. In our household, all I heard was to work hard, and everything would be all right. I never heard the words "go to school" and "college" and "be this or that." Hard work is my family trademark. Even as a teenager and a young child, as far as I can remember, I always worked hard and gave my best. It's what I passed along to my children, and even today, my sons and daughters are hard workers. I remind all who read this book: work hard in whatever you set out to do.

As I grew and journeyed to New York City to work and serve in ministry, I gave it my all and all. While I wasn't doing ministry, I worked outside of ministry. I didn't go back to school after going to New York, so I had to find work to help financially with the ministry. I even stood on street corners and asked for donations for the church with other youth. My brother and I were the youth leaders, and all followed our lead by working hard.

After serving in New York, I was called back to Chicago to help with a new church our leader was opening. I assisted him in ministry there for some years as a young single man. I gave it my all. I found work and still stood on street corners to ask for donations. As the years went by, I yearned for a spouse and a family. As you know, I left the ministry after I met Nita and got married and started a family. Nita and I both had jobs and worked hard for our family. As time went on, our first child came, and the cost of having a family grew. This is when I realized I needed more income to support my family. With only one-half of high school credit, I began to think, *Who would hire me to work without any education?*

My wheels began to turn. *What do I need to do?* I got a second job and started to work on my GED at thirty years old. I worked hard at school and both jobs and still provided for my young family. My foundation of working hard took over. During my first marriage, I earned my GED and BA in liberal arts and got a promotion. Working hard was paying off. Then the divorce happened, and it appeared like it was the end of the road. But it wasn't the end; it was just the beginning of something new that God was preparing me for. It didn't feel like, look like, or sound like God was working. After working hard after the divorce and trying to stay focused and remain rooted in what my dad taught me, I made it through.

Working for the Salvation Army was in God's plan for me. I did leave the Army for a moment, but God brought me back to heal my brokenness and to get me ready for ministry with the corps. During the time with the Army, I was able to continue my education and become an officer and a counselor for officers. At the Army, I also became a board-certified chaplain and earned my doctorate of ministry. I even got ill, lost both kidneys, and almost passed away. But God had a plan for me with the Salvation Army.

In closing, I proudly finished my service with the Army and retired on July 1, 2019. I served as an employee for twenty years and in ministry for twenty years. I served as chaplain, envoy, lieutenant, cadet, captain, and major. I am now still working in ministry as Dr. Williams. Won't God do it?

Lastly, I'd like to say that the shepherd God, who watched over Israel in the Old Testament, watched over me by providing food, shelter, and protection. Even while I was going through my desert experiences, He was there during those hot times. He led me to green pastures. Green pastures were often and far between. It was many days I wondered, *Where was God?* There were many days the Almighty was silent.

When it was too hot and I wasn't able to bear it, He led me to quiet waters. Water revives one in the desert. As a sheep, I couldn't have survived without water, but the shepherd provided for me during those hot and trying times. The shepherd knew how to find the hidden springs and collect the flood waters that rushed down the desert canyons in the winter months.

I got lost many days and months, but the shepherd led me back to the right path. Many paths I have taken in life has seemed very treacherous and steep, but He guided me through them. Yes, I have left the path on me own and gotten lost; yes, I was that one lost sheep. But the shepherd came after me. As the desert is known as a place of intense heat, bright light, darkness, and cold, my life has been the same. Even when I left home at the age of fifteen and my brother was seventeen years old, the shepherd was always there, even when I didn't know. I was led through the valleys of the shadow of death. He brought me through spiritual, emotional, mental, and social effects of grief and loss.

Even still today in the New Testament, Jesus, the Word of God, is the shepherd and is leading and guiding me. He has used the rod and staff to protect me against the enemy. Also, when I was unable to stand and walk, I was able to stand up and walk with His rod and staff. When I was tired and on my last leg, He prepared a table for me to share a meal, in His presence, to comfort me. He showed me His gracious hospitality. Even today, His goodness and mercy are chasing me everywhere I go. I will remain in the house of the Lord forever.

If you don't know the Shepherd, this altar is always available for you; come to Him right now. Ask Him to create in you a clean heart and a right spirit so you can serve Him.

ABOUT THE AUTHOR

Charles is married to Carol Williams in the last twenty-three years and counting. They have no children together. Charles has three children from his first marriage; Carol has one child from her first marriage. Charles's Christian journey began at an early age.

Growing up as a kid, Charles's grandmother took him and his siblings to church. His parents didn't go to church. Charles's grandmother attended a small Church of God in Christ on the West Side of Chicago. He learned about living a Christian life early.

Later at age eight, he and his brothers met a community pastor. His name was Rev. Nelson Brown. The name of the ministry was World Wide Wonders Deliverance. Charles gave his life to Christ at age eight. This ministry had Bible classes weekdays and weekends. Also, they had sports teams to draw the youth of the community.

Later, he was given minister license as a teenager. Charles stay with that ministry until age twenty-four. He traveled with that ministry during revivals in Chicago and other cities. He also moved to New York City for a number of years, helping with the church in Harlem. Sometime later, he came back to Chicago to help with the church there. During a revival at a church on the South Side of Chicago named God's House of Prayer Church of God in Christ, he met Juanita Anderson. Sometime later, they dated and soon got married.

He became a member of her church, God's House of Prayer Church of God in Christ. Elder Jesse Ewing was her pastor. After serving there for one year, they moved on to Outreach Church of God in Christ, where Pastor James Sims was pastor. It's where Charles grew as a man and learned how to be a man and how to care for his family. Some years later, Charles and Juanita began to have problems, which led to divorce. Their marriage produced three children.

Charles was working with the Salvation Army as a computer operator and later as a programmer for twenty years. Being around the Army through those years, he was able to get a firsthand look at how the Army did ministry. After being divorced and single for five years, he met Carol Mckay. He was introduced to Carol by her best friend, Pam Snow, and the rest is history. Charles and Carol became impressed and wanted to be a part of the Salvation Army ministry. So when Carol and Charles got married, each of them had their own church home and pastor.

Charles and Carol decided to leave their churches and come together and serve with the Salvation Army. It was a challenge for the both of them. He attended the Church of God in Christ, which is the world's largest Black church where dancing, shouting, and speaking in tongues happens. It was like a party every service. Carol also attend a large Black church as well where they get baptized by water every service. The Army is a White-born church from England with little emotions.

It took some time for Charles and Carol to get adjusted to their form of service, but they adjusted. The Salvation Army is where Charles earned four degrees. Three of those were funded by them. Charles earned a bachelor of arts (BA), masters in pastoral counseling (MPC), masters of divinity (MDiv), and a doctor of ministry (DMin). Also, he became a board-certified chaplain (BCC). It's where he found his passion and gift of serving hurting people.

All of Charles's degrees along with his life experience made him the man he is today, ready to serve. It's why Dr. Williams wrote this book—to encourage others who seem to have no hope or have lost hope. All in all, he spent forty-two years serving with the Salvation Army: twenty years as employee and twenty-two years in ministry. Charles and Carol retired from the Salvation Army on July 1, 2019.